Nature's Children

PET RABBITS

by Ann Weil

Grolier Educational

FACTS IN BRIEF

Classification of the Rabbit

Class: *Mammalia* (mammals)

Order: *Lagomorpha* (small gnawing mammals with two pairs of upper incisor teeth)

Family: *Leporidae* (rabbits and hares)

Genus: 11 genera

Species: *Oryctolagus cuniculus* (the European common rabbit)

World distribution. Europe, North and South America, Asia, Africa.

Habitat. Indoors or out, in protective hutches that shelter animals from weather and predators.

Distinctive physical characteristics. Long ears, hind legs much longer and stronger than forelegs, short tail, three pairs of incisors (two in upper jaw, one in lower jaw), eyes located at the sides of the head, capable of seeing in every direction.

Habits. Wild rabbits live in family groups. Rabbits are timid and usually come out at dusk and dawn to feed.

Diet. Grasses and other leafy plants, roots, berries, tree bark, pellets, and other pet foods.

Library of Congress Cataloging-in-Publication Data

Weil, Ann, 1960-
    Pet rabbits / Ann Weil.
        p.   cm. — (Nature's children)
    Includes index.
    Summary: Describes distinctive physical characteristics, habitat, behavior, diet, distribution, types, and domestic care required of this animal sometimes used as a pet.
    ISBN 0-7172-9071-9 (hardbound)
    1. Rabbits—Juvenile literature.   [1. Rabbits. 2. Pets.]
I. Title. II. Series
SF453.2.W45 1997
636.9'322—dc21

97-5981
CIP
AC

35, 709 ✳

This library reinforced edition was published in 1997 exclusively by:

 Grolier Educational
Sherman Turnpike, Danbury, Connecticut 06816

Set ISBN 0-7172-7661-9
Pet Rabbits ISBN 0-7172-9071-9

Contents

Few animals are more appealing than the gentle rabbit, with its long ears, twitching nose, and hopping motion. In the wild rabbits are found just about everywhere, from prairies and plains to forests and snowy mountains. But they also are found in homes, farms, and petting zoos.

Domestic, or tame, rabbits are all descended from the European wild rabbit. They vary from two-and-a-half pound (one kilogram) dwarf rabbits to large rabbits the size of a cat. Centuries of domestic breeding have changed these wild creatures into dozens of recognizable breeds with many different colors, sizes, and personalities.

Some breeds are raised for food or fur. But as millions of people have learned, rabbits also make fine pets. They are easy to care for. Even more important, they are affectionate, quiet, and playful companions.

With their long ears and twitching noses rabbits make appealing pets.

Choosing a Rabbit

Some breeds, or types, of rabbits are more suitable to keep as pets than others. Purebred rabbits are those that belong to a particular recognized breed. The best are available from breeders, people who raise rabbits for profit. An animal shelter can be another excellent place to find a pet rabbit. Most shelters have rabbits that are up for adoption, and these animals usually are in good physical condition.

Rabbits are best adopted when two to three months old. This allows them to be given lots of affection and care early in life, which makes them tamer, more responsive pets.

A future owner should be careful to select a healthy rabbit, one that is alert and active, with clean, shiny fur. Its ears should be straight and erect, and its eyes, bright, clear, and dry. Runny noses, lack of energy, and dull-looking fur are signs that an animal may not be in good health.

Rabbits come in many sizes and colors.

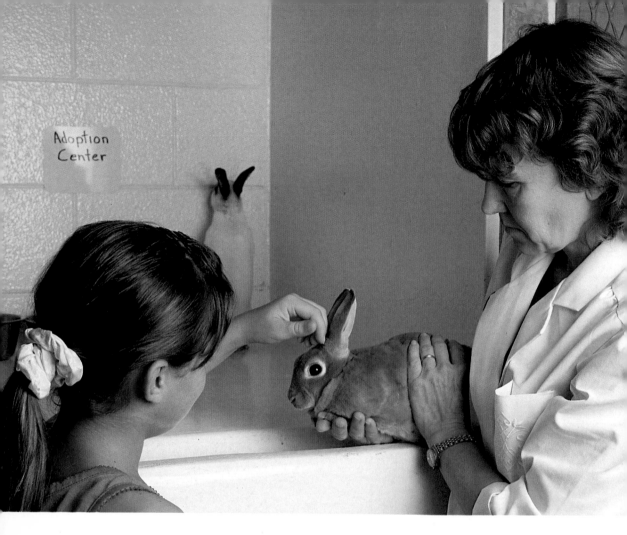

New owners sometimes need help from a vet.

Two's Company

Both bucks (males) and does (females) make good pets. Telling bucks and does apart, however, can be difficult, especially when the animals are young. For this reason, new owners often ask for professional help to determine if their new pet is a male or female rabbit.

Generally, bucks make the best pets. This is mainly because of their disposition, or way of thinking and acting. However, a doe's cage is easier to clean because, unlike the buck, she doesn't mark her territory with urine.

Owners who decide to buy two rabbits should try to get two females. In groups larger than this it is best to have no more than one male. That is because two bucks probably will compete with each other for the right to mate with the does.

The Rabbit Family

Many people think that rabbits are rodents, probably because rabbits have large front teeth like guinea pigs, gerbils, and mice. But rabbits have an extra set of upper incisors, or front teeth. This puts them, along with hares and pikas (short-legged mammals with no visible tails), in their own special order, called Lagomorpha.

People often confuse rabbits and hares. This is not surprising. After all, the Belgian hare is really a rabbit, and the jackrabbit and the snowshoe rabbit are actually hares! Even though hares and rabbits are closely related, they are not the same. Unlike rabbits, hares do not dig burrows, and their young are born fully furred and open-eyed.

Wild rabbits and hares do not make good pets! Once in a while a young, orphaned wild rabbit may adapt to domestic life. But for the most part wild rabbits can never be fully tamed. They are better off left in the wild.

Wild rabbits may look as adorable as domestic ones, but they rarely make good pets.

Popular Breeds

The breed most often sold in pet shops is the medium-sized, white English rabbit. Another popular medium-sized breed is the Dutch belted, or panda, rabbit. It has a wide belt of white fur around the middle and a splash of white on the face. Dutch rabbits are known for their sweet temperaments.

The long-haired Angora is particularly beautiful and friendly. Angoras were first bred for their silky fur, which was used to make sweaters and scarves. Now, however, they are gaining popularity as pets and can be found at most rabbit shows.

The Polish and the Netherland dwarf rabbits are "pocket-sized" breeds weighing only two or three pounds (0.9–1.4 kilograms) each. The Netherland dwarf actually is the smallest domestic rabbit.

Polish rabbits are usually white with ruby-red eyes, but they can also be black and tan with sapphire-blue eyes. When a magician pulls a rabbit from a hat, it probably is a Polish rabbit.

The white Polish rabbit, with its ruby-red eyes, is a favorite of magicians.

Other Breeds

Himalayan and Californian rabbits are two other popular breeds. Himalayans weigh between three and five pounds (1.4–2.3 kilograms); Californians are medium-sized rabbits weighing about nine pounds (4 kilograms). Both have beautiful white coats set off by black noses, ears, tails, and feet.

Although it is actually a rabbit, the Belgian hare gets its name because it is big, long, and lanky, like a hare. The Flemish giant, another common breed, is the largest of all domestic rabbits. It can weigh up to fifteen pounds (7 kilograms).

An unusual breed is the lop-eared rabbit. Over the years these have been bred to have extraordinarily long ears. Unfortunately, the breeders may have gone too far. The ears of some of these rabbits drag all the way to the ground! Lop-ears require special care and are not recommended as pets.

Pocket-sized dwarf rabbits make unusual pets.

Home Sweet Hutch

Rabbits need comfortable, enclosed hutches, or rabbit houses, to live in. Solitary by nature, each rabbit should have its own hutch.

A typical hutch for a pet rabbit is simply a wooden or metal frame box, with ceiling, walls, and floor made of wire mesh. The hutch should have a hinged door, and the top should lift off for easier cleaning. Pet suppliers usually keep a variety of hutches in stock. A homemade hutch is fine, too, and it can be easy—and fun—to build.

Since rabbits prefer privacy, each hutch should have a separate, enclosed "bedroom" area. Rabbits have a fondness for soft bedding, so some should always be provided. Hay is best, but shredded paper, straw, or peat moss will do nicely.

A metal-framed hutch makes an excellent home for a pet rabbit.

Indoor Rabbits

It is important for pet rabbits to exercise outside their hutches. But before a rabbit can be let loose in the home, owners must first rabbit-proof the area. This means that things that can be chewed should be put away—or kept out of reach. (Rabbits are curious by nature and will gnaw anything in sight.) Electrical wires, in particular, pose a serious threat for these pets.

A pet rabbit who has the run of the house usually needs only a small hutch, since it is used only for sleeping. The door of the hutch should be left open to allow the rabbit to get to its food and water. Indoor hutches usually include a bottom tray or some sheets of recycled newspaper to catch droppings.

Like house cats, pet rabbits are easy to litter train. Owners should simply place a separate litter box inside the hutch and then place some of the rabbit's droppings into the box. A smart rabbit will be litter trained in just a few weeks.

Outdoor Rabbits

Pet rabbits do not have to be kept indoors. They also can lead happy, healthy lives outside the house. An outdoor hutch should be two to three feet (60 to 90 centimeters) off the ground, safe from other animals. It should have a slanted roof and an overhang to keep rain from dripping inside.

Rabbits need fresh air and sunshine, but they also need to be protected from harsh weather. Hutches should not be placed in a drafty area or in direct sunlight. Likely places for a hutch might be in a shed or barn, a porch with an overhang, or even a garage. On very hot days it also helps to freeze a plastic bottle of water to place in the hutch. The rabbit will keep cool by lying next to the icy bottle!

Finally, rabbits love "playpens," portable running pens made from light wood and wire mesh. These pens need only a top and sides—the grass becomes the floor. Inside the pen rabbits can nibble the grass and get plenty of sunshine, exercise, and fresh air.

Getting Along with Other Family Pets

Even in homes with other family pets, free-roaming rabbits seem to fit in quite easily. Perhaps this is because they are quiet and never seem to threaten or annoy other animals. Mature cats and dogs soon lose interest and leave the rabbits alone. On the other hand, kittens and puppies will adopt the rabbit as a playmate.

Neighboring cats and dogs, however, are another story. To them the rabbit is not a pet; it is prey. As a result, the rabbit may be chased or perhaps even harmed—or worse. Because of this pet rabbits must be watched carefully whenever they are outdoors.

Even pet rabbits enjoy getting outdoors in the fresh air and sunshine.

Rabbit Care

Pet rabbits need fresh food and clean water daily. Their cages must be kept clean too. Rabbits are clean animals and appreciate a neat hutch. Moreover, clean hutches help protect rabbits from illness.

Soiled bedding should be removed from the hutch and replaced with fresh material. Once a week the hutch should be scrubbed. However, an owner should not clean the cage while the rabbit is in it because the animal will see this as an invasion of its territory.

Rabbits enjoy attention, so petting them is a sure way to make them happy. But rabbits should not be overly handled. They become tired and even sick if they are picked up and played with too often.

Never pick up a rabbit by its ears! The correct way to lift a rabbit is to scoop it up with one hand at the nape (or scruff) of the neck and the other hand beneath its hindquarters. Rabbits' ears have delicate muscles and membranes and should never be mishandled.

Rabbits should be held firmly and gently— and never by the ears!

Grooming

Most rabbits take care of their own grooming. Angoras and other longhaired breeds, however, need to be combed often with a wire brush in order to keep their long hair clean and untangled.

Rabbit owners often find themselves getting scratched by the creatures' toenails. To avoid being scratched, owners should clip their pets' toenails. This will also help protect owners' rugs, furniture, and other belongings.

When trimming a rabbit's nails, care must be taken not to clip the nails too short. If too much of the nail is taken off, the blood vessel at the base of the nail can get cut and bleed. Happily, the wound looks much worse than it really is. Still, many owners seek out professional groomers for this messy task.

Long-haired rabbits like this one need special—
and frequent—brushing and grooming.

Rabbit Health

In general, rabbits are healthy animals. Most of their health problems are due to simple causes. Bad feeding, lack of exercise, and overcrowding in the hutch are three of the most common. Rabbits also can get bacterial infections from dirty hutches, and exposure to cold drafts and rain can bring on illness as well.

Owners should always be on the alert for any sign of illness. A rabbit that is listless (not energetic), one that has a runny nose, or one that refuses to eat might be sick.

At the first sign of illness the rabbit in question should be separated from others. If in an hour or two the rabbit seems to be getting worse, a veterinarian should be called at once. A rabbit's health can go downhill very quickly! For proper treatment owners should consult a qualified vet who is experienced with rabbits.

Prevention is the most important part of keeping rabbits from getting sick. Owners who provide good food, plenty of fresh water, and a clean cage usually will have healthy rabbits.

Owners should check over their pet rabbits often for any sign of illness.

Common Ailments

There are several common ailments, or sicknesses, that can affect pet rabbits.

Diarrhea usually is caused by eating too much green food. A veterinarian should be consulted immediately. Treated early, diarrhea is not a major problem. But in severe cases it can be fatal.

Scratches or cuts should be cleaned immediately and then treated with sulfate ointment or powder. Deep holes or very bad cuts and scrapes should be cared for by a veterinarian.

Snuffles are like a cold in humans. The symptoms include sneezing and watery eyes. An antibiotic (by prescription only) mixed in water often clears up a rabbit's snuffles.

Weepy eye usually comes from an infection of the eyelids. It is easily treated with eyedrops or ointments that can be obtained from a veterinarian.

Indoor rabbits that have the run of the house can wander—or even nap—wherever they please!

Rabbit Food

Did you know that rabbits eat their food twice? Sometime after eating, rabbits produce soft, partly digested droppings, which they proceed to eat. (This is usually done early in the morning.) Later in the day they produce hard droppings, which they do not eat. This unusual process helps rabbits get the full nutrition from each meal.

Rabbits need a variety of different foods, including pellets, hay, and fresh vegetables. Commercial food pellets, which are available at most pet and feed stores, contain corn, oats, soybean mix, alfalfa, vitamins, and minerals. Due to their delicate digestive systems, rabbits also need foods rich in fiber, such as hay. They should not be fed cabbage, lettuce, or asparagus. Rabbits also need something to gnaw on, such as carrots or strong green twigs. And like all pets, rabbits must have plenty of cool, fresh water.

*Vegetables can be an important addition to
a pet rabbit's diet.*

To Breed or Not to Breed

Rabbit breeding is a hobby enjoyed by thousands of people. Choosing animals to breed, trying to breed the best possible individuals, and watching the baby rabbits grow can all be fascinating fun.

On the other hand, successful breeding requires time, effort, and planning. After all, each adult rabbit will need its own hutch, and breeders need time and money to care for all the rabbits that live under their roofs. It is no wonder that for many rabbit owners, one or two are enough!

It is a good idea for owners to keep breeding records. In this way they can determine which buck is the best for fathering litters and which doe produces the healthiest offspring.

Breeding rabbits can be interesting and fun—but it can mean lots and lots of rabbits!

The Mating Game

Until the owner is ready to breed them, the buck and does should be kept in separate hutches. Knowledgeable rabbit owners wait until a doe is about eight months old before mating it with a buck. At that age the doe should be placed in the buck's hutch, not the other way around. Female rabbits are quite territorial, which means that they will protect an area they believe to be theirs. As a result, does are not often friendly to other rabbits that enter their space.

Once the two become friendly, the doe is allowed to stay in the buck's hutch for a few hours and then returned to her own hutch. This process may need to be repeated several times until mating occurs.

Approximately 31 days after the doe successfully mates she will give birth to her litter. Six babies are normal for a litter, but rabbits can have as many as ten offspring at a time.

Baby rabbits grow quickly on their mother's rich milk.

Baby rabbits—like these young lop-eared ones—
cling to their mothers.

Pregnancy

A pregnant doe must have a nesting box in her hutch. This is just an open-topped box about 18 inches (46 centimeters) square and 9 inches (23 centimeters) high. The box should be filled with clean, soft bedding.

About a week before the doe kindles, or gives birth, she will pull some soft fur from her belly to make her own nest inside the box. This fur makes an ultrasoft nest for her babies. It also exposes the mother's nipples so the babies will be able to nurse.

Rabbits usually give birth at night. It is best to leave the doe alone during this time—and even for a few days afterward. If overly disturbed, the new mother might desert or even destroy her own offspring.

Baby Rabbits

At birth rabbits are tiny and have no fur. Their eyes and ears are sealed shut. But the young bunnies grow very fast. At two weeks they have a full coat of fur, ears that stand up straight, and they open their eyes. Soon the youngsters can hop around the hutch and even steal their mother's food.

At six to eight weeks the young rabbits can be weaned from their mother's milk. This is done by simply feeding them rabbit pellets and milk diluted with an equal part of water. At the age of two months the young rabbits can be moved to their own hutch.

Finally, when the young rabbits are three or four months old, the bucks and does should be separated. This is done to prevent any accidental breeding.

By the time they are two weeks old, young rabbits have fur, ears that stand up, and opened eyes.

Show Time

Shows and competitions are a source of fun for many rabbit owners. Going to rabbit shows can help owners learn more about their pets. It also can help them meet other people who share their interest in rabbits.

Some shows are open only to purebred rabbits. These shows are often supervised by the American Rabbit Breeders Association (ARBA). Other shows, especially those at county fairs, are open to any and all pet rabbits.

At shows rabbits are judged on their general health, coloring, form, ears, eyes—EVERYTHING. Judges look to see whether a particular rabbit fits the generally accepted standard for its breed. If they spot anything unusual, even a few stray hairs of the wrong color or a strange-looking toenail, the rabbit will probably not be awarded a prize.

Rabbits stay in their hutches during most competitions and shows.

When Owners Are Away

Even when they are away from home, concerned owners make sure their pet rabbits are well cared for during their absence. Usually good friends, relatives, or neighbors are happy to help out.

"Rabbit-sitters" should be introduced to the pets beforehand. Owners should provide written instructions about everything the rabbits will need, including food, water, and cage cleaning, and also review these lists with the sitters.

Before owners go away, they should make an inventory, or tally, of supplies. Is plenty of food and bedding on hand? What about vitamins, medicines, and anything else the rabbit might need? After all, this would not be the time to run out of necessities!

Anything else? Just in case of an emergency, the sitter should be furnished two important phone numbers—the owner's and the vet's.

Rabbits We Know and Love

Three of the most popular rabbits are not even real animals! Just the mention of their names—the Easter Bunny, Peter Rabbit, and Bugs Bunny—can bring instant smiles to millions of faces. The Easter Bunny is a legendary holiday animal whose origins go back as far as ancient Egypt. Today many young children are taught that the Easter Bunny brings eggs at Easter. Still popular today are the familiar traditions of hunting for Easter eggs and rolling Easter eggs.

Peter Rabbit is the title character in a 1902 children's book by Beatrix Potter. He first appeared in 1893 in an illustrated letter written by Potter to amuse a friend's five-year-old son.

Bugs Bunny is a cartoon character created in the early 1940s. Many talented people made contributions to the drawings, voice, and stories, and because of their efforts Bugs's personality has won him fans the world over. After all, who wouldn't love a rabbit who asks the familiar question, "What's up, Doc?"

Abandoned Pets: A Problem

At Easter and on other holidays adorable baby rabbits are often sold as pets. Unfortunately, many of these rabbits are too young to be taken away from their mothers, and they die after a short time in their new homes.

There is also a problem, though, with the little rabbits that do survive. Many of the same people who once considered the bunnies so cute no longer want them as adult pets. Sometimes these people set their unwanted pets "free" in the woods. But it is very difficult for tame animals to survive in the wild. They simply do not know how.

Luckily, however, many people would never dream of abandoning a pet. Committed rabbit owners know that having a pet is a big responsibility.

A pet rabbit is a big responsibility . . . but it also is a source of joy and affection.

Rabbits in Legend and Lore

Rabbits and hares have figured in myths, legends, and tales all around the world. In Africa hares are a symbol of cleverness. In South America people once worshipped a mythical creature called the Great Hare. It was, they believed, the creator of the universe. There is also the ancient Greek tale of the tortoise and the hare. In it the swift-running hare is so vain and lazy that it loses a race to the slow-moving tortoise.

A familiar tradition involving rabbits is the belief that a rabbit's foot will bring good luck. Because of this people have been carrying rabbit's feet with them for hundreds of years. According to a similar superstition, if you take a rabbit's foot into a churchyard at midnight when the moon is full, it will shield you from evil forever.

What do you suppose a rabbit might think about that?

Words to Know

Angora   A breed of longhaired rabbit.

Breeder   Someone who raises rabbits for profit.

Buck   A male rabbit.

Doe   A female rabbit.

Hare   An animal closely related to rabbits.

Hutch   A cage for rabbits.

Kindle   To give birth to young rabbits.

Litter   The young rabbits in one birth.

Nesting box   An enclosed area in a doe's hutch where she will give birth to and raise a litter.

Pellets   Commercial concentrated dry feed for rabbits.

Purebred   A rabbit of a recognized breed.

Wean   To begin feeding young rabbits solid food instead of their mother's milk.

INDEX

Cover Photo: SuperStock, Inc.
Photo Credits: Norvia Behling (Behling & Johnson Photography), pages 8, 17, 20, 22, 25, 26, 29, 35, 39, 41, 45; Dick Keen (Unicorn Stock Photos), page 14; Lynn M. Stone, pages 4, 7, 31, 36; SuperStock, Inc., pages 11, 13, 33.